AF483759

VIVEKANANDA'S VIRTUES

A BLUEPRINT FOR MODERN LIVING

DR. MINAKSHI BANSAL

Copyright © Dr. Minakshi Bansal
All Rights Reserved.

This book has been self-published with all reasonable efforts taken to make the material error-free by the author. No part of this book shall be used, reproduced in any manner whatsoever without written permission from the author, except in the case of brief quotations embodied in critical articles and reviews.

The Author of this book is solely responsible and liable for its content including but not limited to the views, representations, descriptions, statements, information, opinions and references ["Content"]. The Content of this book shall not constitute or be construed or deemed to reflect the opinion or expression of the Publisher or Editor. Neither the Publisher nor Editor endorse or approve the Content of this book or guarantee the reliability, accuracy or completeness of the Content published herein and do not make any representations or warranties of any kind, express or implied, including but not limited to the implied warranties of merchantability, fitness for a particular purpose. The Publisher and Editor shall not be liable whatsoever for any errors, omissions, whether such errors or omissions result from negligence, accident, or any other cause or claims for loss or damages of any kind, including without limitation, indirect or consequential loss or damage arising out of use, inability to use, or about the reliability, accuracy or sufficiency of the information contained in this book.

Made with ♥ on the Notion Press Platform
www.notionpress.com

DEDICATION

This book is dedicated to all who seek to transcend the ordinary, to those who strive to lead lives enriched with purpose and compassion. It is for the seekers of wisdom, the champions of virtue, and the believers in the innate potential of every human soul to manifest greatness. May the timeless teachings of Swami Vivekananda inspire you to illuminate the world with your spirit and actions.

ɔɔɔ

Contents

Contents

Contents

Prayer

"Om Bhadram Karnebhih Shrinuyama Devah
Bhadram Pashyemakshabhiryajatrah
Sthirairangais Tushtuvamsastanubhih
Vyashema Devahitam Yadayuh
Svasti Na Indro Vriddhashravah
Svasti Nah Pusha Vishwavedah
Svasti Nastarkshyo Arishtanemih
Svasti No Brihaspatir Dadhatu
Om Shantih Shantih Shantih"

This mantra is a prayer for universal well-being, invoking the blessings of various deities for protection, health, and happiness. It emphasizes the importance of experiencing the auspicious through all senses and living a life aligned with divine purpose. The repetition of "Shantih" at the end signifies a deep desire for peace in the individual, the environment, and the universe at large. This mantra is often recited as a prayer for peace, prosperity, and the physical and spiritual well-being of all beings.

ᐅᐅᐅ

About The Author

Dr. Minakshi Bansal, born in the bustling metropolis of Delhi, India, has led a life steeped in artistry, scholarly pursuit, and an unwavering commitment to societal betterment. Following her marriage, she relocated to Ahmedabad, Gujarat, where she has since blossomed into a multifaceted beacon of inspiration for many. Dr. Minakshi is not only recognized as a gifted artist in the realm of Fine Arts but also as an esteemed author, a devoted social worker and a dedicated research scholar in Psychology. Her journey, marked by a profound dedication to elevating those around her, especially the downtrodden and underprivileged children of society, is a testament to her deep-seated belief in the transformative power of engagement and empathy.

From her earliest days, Minakshi was distinguished by an insatiable appetite for reading. Her literary universe was inhabited by characters and narratives that spanned ethical tales, motivational and inspirational stories, and the mythic parables imbued with life lessons. This voracious reading habit was not merely for personal edification but was driven by a desire to distill and disseminate the essence of these narratives to foster the development of students and peers alike. She was particularly captivated by the lives and teachings of historical figures and spiritual leaders such as Adi Shankaracharya, Swami Vivekananda, Dr. APJ Abdul Kalam, Mahamana Pandit Madan Mohan Malviya, Mahatma Gandhi, Sardar Vallabhai Patel, and Vinoba Bhave, among others. Their philosophies and life stories fueled her ambition to embody their ideals of resilience, selflessness, and relentless pursuit of knowledge.

Dr. Minakshi's academic and practical engagement with psychology has been equally noteworthy. As a research scholar, her focus has been on exploring the intricate tapestry of the human psyche, aiming to unlock the potential for psychological well-being and societal harmony. Her scholarly work is complemented by her active involvement in social work, where she employs her academic insights to make tangible differences in the lives of the underprivileged. Her endeavours in social work are characterized by an innovative approach that combines traditional wisdom with contemporary psychological practices to address the multifaceted challenges faced by these communities.

Her artistic talents, another facet of her diverse capabilities, are not merely a personal passion but also serve as a medium through which she communicates and connects with others. Her art, rich in symbolism and emotional depth, reflects her philosophical inquiries and social concerns, offering viewers a glimpse into the breadth of her intellect and the depth of her compassion.

In addition to her contributions to the arts and social sciences, Dr. Minakshi has embraced the healing arts of Pranic Healing, mastering the techniques developed by Master Choa Kok Sui. This practice, which focuses on the manipulation of Prana or life energy to heal the body and aura, has been both a personal journey of discovery and a means through which she extends her healing touch to others. Her proficiency in Pranic Healing is complemented by her advocacy and teaching of various forms of meditation aimed at rejuvenation, personal betterment, and the cultivation of harmony within individuals and communities alike.

Dr. Minakshi's life is a narrative of relentless pursuit, not just of personal achievement but of the upliftment and empowerment of society at large. Her diverse interests and talents—spanning the arts, literature, psychology, and the healing practices—converge on a singular path of service. She embodies the spirit of the luminaries who inspired her, channelling their legacy through her actions and teachings. Through her books, art, and social initiatives, she continues to inspire a new generation to embark on their own journeys of self-discovery, resilience, and altruism.

Her commitment to social betterment, particularly her focus on uplifting underprivileged children, reflects a deep understanding of the transformative potential of education and personal development. By integrating her knowledge of psychology, her artistic sensibilities, and her healing practices, Dr. Bansal has developed a holistic approach to social work that addresses both the immediate needs and the long-term well-being of the communities she serves.

As an author, Dr. Minakshi's writings offer a blend of inspirational insights, practical wisdom, and reflective contemplations drawn from her extensive reading and life experiences. Her books serve as a guide for those seeking to navigate the complexities of life with grace, resilience, and purpose. Through her narratives, she extends an invitation to her readers to explore the depths of their own potential and to contribute meaningfully to the collective well-being of society.

In Dr. Minakshi Bansal, we find a remarkable synthesis of the artist, the scholar, the healer, and the social activist. Her life's work stands as a beacon of hope and a source of inspiration for individuals seeking to make a difference in the world. Her story is a compelling reminder of the power of individual action, rooted in compassion and driven by a profound commitment to the betterment of humanity. Dr. Minakshi's legacy is not just in the tangible outcomes of her efforts but in the enduring spirit of inquiry, empathy, and service that she embodies.

ৡৡৡ

Preface

In this book, we delve into the profound teachings of Swami Vivekananda, whose insights into human nature and spirituality continue to illuminate paths for personal growth and societal harmony. Vivekananda, a spiritual beacon of the 19th century, has left an indelible mark on the philosophy of modern living. His principles offer not just a philosophical perspective, but practical applications that can foster a life of fulfillment and purpose in the contemporary world.

Vivekananda's teachings emerge from a deep understanding of ancient Indian spiritual traditions, yet they resonate strikingly with modern global challenges. He advocated for values such as self-reliance, integrity, and service, seeing them as essential for personal excellence and social welfare. In a world increasingly driven by material success and rapid technological advancement, his call for a balanced life that honors spiritual integrity and ethical conduct is more relevant than ever.

This book aims to present Vivekananda's virtues as practical elements that can be integrated into the fabric of everyday life. Each chapter explores a different virtue, examining its relevance and application in today's context. From cultivating self-belief and embracing diversity to the power of education and the significance of service, the chapters provide a comprehensive look at how these timeless principles can guide us in navigating the complexities of modern life.

The journey through Vivekananda's teachings begins with an exploration of self-belief, a cornerstone of his philosophy. Vivekananda asserted that faith in oneself is the secret of greatness. In a world where self-doubt and insecurity often cloud our potential, understanding and embracing one's own capabilities can be transformative.

Furthermore, the principle of unity in diversity, which Vivekananda championed fervently, offers a crucial lesson in coexistence and respect for our globalized, multicultural world. As societies become more diverse, the ability to see unity in diversity becomes essential for social harmony and peace.

Education as a tool for liberation is another key theme of Vivekananda's teachings that we explore. He viewed education not just as a means of intellectual development, but as the key to moral and spiritual growth. For Vivekananda, true education empowers individuals, frees them from ignorance, and instills a sense of duty toward society.

In discussing the role of women in society, Vivekananda's ideas on women's empowerment and leadership are profoundly progressive. He believed that no society could progress without improving the situation of women, emphasizing their education and participation in public life as crucial for societal advancement.

The book also delves into how Vivekananda's virtues can enhance personal and professional lives. For instance, his teachings on overcoming obstacles with grace, and maintaining harmony between mind and body, provide valuable strategies for managing personal challenges and health.

In terms of community and leadership, Vivekananda advocated for a style of leadership rooted in ethics and selflessness. This book examines how these ideas can reshape contemporary approaches to leadership and community engagement, proposing a model where leaders are not just administrators, but visionaries who inspire and uplift their communities.

Kindness and generosity, as discussed by Vivekananda, are not just moral choices but essential for cultivating a fulfilling life. These chapters highlight how acts of kindness and generosity enrich the giver and the receiver, creating a more compassionate society.

Lastly, the book addresses the need for a visionary outlook, which Vivekananda emphasized for personal and social advancement. His teachings encourage us to look beyond immediate circumstances and work towards greater goals that benefit not only ourselves but also the broader community.

By revisiting and reinterpreting Vivekananda's teachings, this book aims to provide readers with a blueprint for modern living that is both meaningful and practical. It is designed to help readers navigate their personal and professional challenges with wisdom, strength, and compassion, inspired by one of the greatest philosophers and spiritual leaders of our time.

It is a call to action to revive and implement age-old wisdom in ways that resonate with and address the demands and challenges of modern life. Through this book, readers will discover how Vivekananda's timeless teachings can be applied to cultivate a life of greater purpose, happiness, and harmony.

Dr. Minakshi Bansal
Social Activist
Ahmedabad, Gujarat, Bharat

ppp

ONE

THE POWER OF SELF-BELIEF – UNDERSTANDING VIVEKANANDA'S TEACHINGS ON SELF-CONFIDENCE

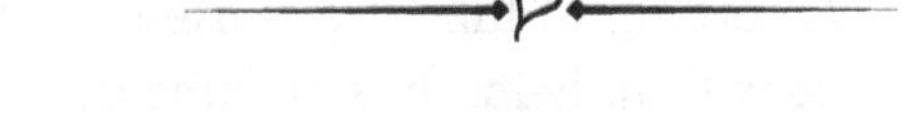

Swami Vivekananda, a profound spiritual leader and thinker, emphasized the power of self-belief as a cornerstone for personal and societal growth. His teachings on self-confidence were not merely philosophical musings but practical strategies aimed at empowering individuals, particularly women, to realize their full potential. By exploring his insights, we can uncover timeless principles that are especially relevant in today's context of women empowerment.

Vivekananda believed that self-confidence stemmed from the recognition of one's own divinity. He often quoted the Vedantic idea that each soul is potentially divine, and the goal is to manifest this divinity within by controlling nature, both external and internal. This notion places immense power in the hands of an individual, suggesting that the realization of one's capabilities and strengths is fundamentally a spiritual journey. For women, this is a particularly potent message, confronting social and systemic barriers that often diminish self-worth.

Central to Vivekananda's teachings is the concept of 'Atman', the inner self. He encouraged individuals to look inward and discover the Atman, which is a source of infinite strength and confidence. This introspective process requires one to rise above the superficial judgments of society and to recognize their intrinsic worth and abilities. In a world where women's value is often measured by external standards—be it beauty, age, or roles—the idea of grounding one's confidence in the unchanging, eternal self is revolutionary.

Moreover, Vivekananda championed the idea of fearlessness, which is intrinsically linked to self-confidence. He asserted that fear is one of the greatest enemies of humanity and that it arises from a lack of belief in oneself. According to him, the fearless are those who have faith in the divine within themselves, making them invincible in the face of adversity. For women, this message is empowering, as it encourages them to confront societal challenges, be it discrimination, inequality, or injustice, with a fearless spirit rooted in self-belief.

Vivekananda also saw education as a critical tool for cultivating self-confidence. He argued that education should go beyond mere academic learning to include the development of moral values and self-esteem. Education, according to him, should empower individuals to stand on their own feet, think independently, and question societal norms that are unjust. This perspective on education is particularly relevant for women's empowerment, advocating for a learning process that nurtures self-assurance and critical thinking skills.

Furthermore, Vivekananda's emphasis on practical Vedanta suggests that spirituality need not be confined to the realm of contemplation but should be action-oriented. He believed that true religious practice involves asserting one's potential and working vigorously towards personal and social upliftment. This active approach to spirituality encourages women to engage with the world confidently, contribute meaningfully to societal change, and not retreat into passivity.

The spiritual leader also placed significant emphasis on the strength that comes from unity. He noted that bringing together individuals who are self-confident amplifies their power to effect change. This is particularly relevant for women, as it suggests that when they join hands, believing in their collective strength and divine nature, they can transform society.

In his numerous lectures and writings, Vivekananda consistently highlighted the importance of self-reliance. He encouraged individuals, especially women, to depend on themselves for their development and liberation. This self-reliance is not just about economic independence but also about intellectual and emotional autonomy.

Vivekananda's perspective on self-belief and self-confidence transcends his era, offering a blueprint for modern living that empowers women to navigate their challenges. By embracing his teachings, women can cultivate a robust sense of self that stands unaffected by external validations and societal limitations. In essence, Vivekananda's call to recognize and realize one's divine nature is a call to every woman to see herself as a reservoir of strength, capable of greatness and deserving of respect.

Thus, the teachings of Swami Vivekananda on self-confidence not only provide a spiritual foundation for personal growth but also act as a catalyst for societal transformation, particularly in the empowerment of women. His insights encourage a reevaluation of how self-belief is understood and practiced, promising a pathway to empowerment that is both profound and practical.

TWO

Unity in Diversity – Embracing differences through compassion and empathy

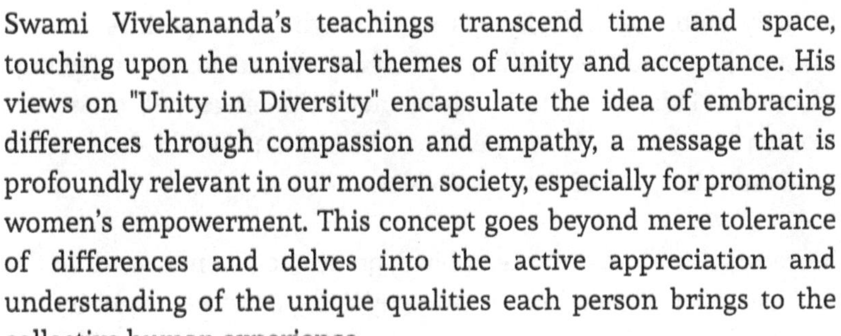

Swami Vivekananda's teachings transcend time and space, touching upon the universal themes of unity and acceptance. His views on "Unity in Diversity" encapsulate the idea of embracing differences through compassion and empathy, a message that is profoundly relevant in our modern society, especially for promoting women's empowerment. This concept goes beyond mere tolerance of differences and delves into the active appreciation and understanding of the unique qualities each person brings to the collective human experience.

Vivekananda believed that the source of all miseries in the world lies in thinking of differences, and from these differences spring all the personal and communal conflicts that plague society. He championed the cause of seeing beyond superficial divisions—those of race, religion, gender, and socioeconomic status—to acknowledge the underlying unity of all humanity. This vision is particularly vital when considering the role of women in society, as it advocates for an environment where their diverse contributions are recognized and celebrated rather than marginalized.

At the heart of Vivekananda's discourse on unity is the principle of Vedantic universalism—the idea that all life is interconnected through an omnipresent divinity. This worldview fosters a deep-seated respect for diversity because it recognizes that diversity itself is an expression of the Divine. By adopting this perspective, individuals can cultivate a profound empathy for others, understanding their feelings, thoughts, and experiences as intimately connected to their own. For women, this empathy is both a tool for navigating their diverse roles in society and a strategy for overcoming the barriers of discrimination and inequality.

Vivekananda also saw empathy and compassion as essential qualities for spiritual and social progress. He often spoke about the importance of 'feeling with' the other, not just 'feeling for' them. This distinction highlights the deeper level of engagement required to truly embrace diversity. It's not enough to sympathize from a distance; one must be willing to understand and share the feelings of others. This empathetic engagement challenges all, especially women, to break down personal biases and build bridges of understanding across various divides.

Moreover, Vivekananda's emphasis on service to mankind as the highest form of worship ties directly into his views on unity. He argued that service rooted in compassion and empathy could unite the most diverse communities by focusing on common human needs and aspirations.

Through service, women find a powerful avenue for leadership and transformation, impacting not just their immediate communities but contributing to global unity.

Education plays a crucial role in cultivating a mindset that values diversity and practices empathy. Vivekananda advocated for an education system that not only imparts knowledge but also molds the character, teaching respect for all life, and appreciation for diversity.

An educational approach that incorporates these values can empower women by providing them with the tools to challenge societal stereotypes and to promote inclusivity and unity.

In practice, embracing diversity through compassion and empathy requires a shift in societal attitudes and structures. It involves creating spaces that actively celebrate differences and promote inclusivity.

For women, this means advocating for policies and practices that acknowledge and address the specific challenges faced by women of different backgrounds and experiences.

Furthermore, Vivekananda's message inspires a collective movement towards a more cohesive society where every individual, regardless of gender, has the opportunity to thrive.

By fostering an environment where differences are embraced rather than feared, society can harness the full potential of its diverse population. Women, empowered by the strength of their diversity, become pivotal to this transformation, leading efforts that weave the rich tapestry of human experience into a unified whole.

Thus, Vivekananda's teachings on unity in diversity are not just philosophical ideals but actionable insights that call for a revolution in how we perceive and interact with one another.

By championing empathy and compassion, these teachings offer a blueprint for a society where diversity is not just accepted but is seen as a vital component of the collective human strength. For women, this translates into a more empowered and equitable standing in society, where they can lead and influence with integrity and respect for all.

ϷϷϷ

THREE

EDUCATION AS LIBERATION – HOW KNOWLEDGE FREES US FROM SOCIETAL CONSTRAINTS

Swami Vivekananda's perspective on education is profound and transformative, emphasizing its role not merely as a process of acquiring information, but as a tool of liberation from societal constraints. He posited that true education should liberate a person from within, freeing them from the shackles of ignorance, prejudice, and limiting societal norms, particularly those that bind women in restrictive roles.

Vivekananda believed that the primary purpose of education should be to foster the growth of an individual's character and intellect, enabling them to stand on their own feet. This concept is especially powerful for women, for whom education can be a direct path to empowerment. By gaining knowledge and developing critical thinking skills, women can challenge and redefine the roles that society has traditionally imposed on them, advocating for their rights and participating more fully in society's economic, political, and cultural life.

According to Vivekananda, education is the manifestation of perfection already in humans. This idea suggests that education should help individuals realize their inherent potential. For women, this is particularly relevant as it challenges the deep-seated societal beliefs about their capabilities and roles. Education enables women to discover and develop their inner strengths and talents, which can lead to a reassessment of their value and contribution to society.

Vivekananda's advocacy for practical and value-based education is crucial. He argued that education should be life-building, man-making, character-making assimilation of ideas. He stressed that education should equip individuals with the ability to think independently and act responsibly, which are critical skills for breaking free from societal constraints. For women, practical education means learning skills that are directly applicable to improving their living conditions and enhancing their decision-making power within their families and communities.

Moreover, Vivekananda placed a strong emphasis on moral education. By cultivating virtues such as honesty, courage, and compassion, education develops the moral backbone of individuals, allowing them to challenge unjust structures and practices in society. This moral foundation is particularly significant for women as it empowers them to challenge injustices like discrimination and inequality that they may face in their daily lives.

Education also promotes social mobility, which is a critical aspect of liberation. By providing women with educational opportunities, they can improve their socioeconomic status, which in turn, provides them with the means to escape cycles of poverty and dependence. Educated women are more likely to participate in the workforce, gain economic independence, and influence societal norms and policies that affect their lives.

Furthermore, Vivekananda believed that education should not be confined to the walls of a classroom but should include learning from the world at large. This idea of education encourages women to engage with and learn from various experiences and cultures, broadening their perspectives and enabling them to transcend parochial viewpoints and practices.

The liberating power of education as described by Vivekananda also involves fostering an environment where questioning and innovation are encouraged. This environment is crucial for societal progress and is particularly empowering for women, who often face traditional restrictions on their behavior and expressions. Educational settings that encourage questioning and critical analysis empower women to challenge and change the discriminatory norms that constrain them.

Education also serves as a bridge that connects diverse people, fostering understanding and reducing prejudices that are often the basis of societal constraints. Through education, women learn about different cultures, religions, and worldviews, which can foster a more inclusive perspective and reduce the biases that fuel discrimination and inequality.

Vivekananda's vision of education as a tool for liberation is deeply relevant today as it addresses fundamental issues of gender equality and women's empowerment. By focusing on the development of the whole person and not just academic achievement, education can transform the lives of women, freeing them from societal constraints and enabling them to pursue their dreams and aspirations.

Thus, in the philosophy of Vivekananda, education emerges not just as a means of personal development, but as a powerful instrument of social change and liberation. For women around the world, education represents a critical pathway out of subjugation and into roles of leadership and influence, fundamentally altering the fabric of society for the better. In essence, education, as envisioned by Vivekananda, does not just shape minds; it liberates them, setting the foundation for a society where every woman can live freely and fully.

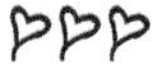

FOUR

The Role of Women in Society – Vivekananda's vision of Women as Nation Builders

Swami Vivekananda's vision for women was revolutionary, particularly in the context of the late 19th and early 20th centuries when women's roles were predominantly confined to the domestic sphere. He saw women as essential nation builders, whose empowerment and participation in societal development were crucial for the progress of any country. His ideas challenge the traditional constraints imposed on women and offer a blueprint for their active participation in nation-building.

Vivekananda's advocacy for women's rights was rooted in his profound belief in the equality of all souls. He frequently referenced the ancient Indian scriptures which held women in high esteem, arguing that a society that does not respect its women cannot progress. According to him, the real measure of a nation's progress is the status it grants to its women. This perspective was not only progressive but also practical, highlighting the untapped potential of half the population.

He strongly believed that education was the key to empowering women, enabling them to contribute effectively to society. For Vivekananda, education was not just about imparting knowledge but about building character and fostering moral values. He argued that educating women was doubly beneficial, as it would impact the family and, by extension, the larger community. Educated women could raise better citizens, thus playing a direct role in nation-building.

Furthermore, Vivekananda criticized the societal norms that kept women ignorant and dependent. He challenged these conventions, advocating for women's access to all the means that would allow them to be independent and self-sufficient. This independence was not seen merely in economic terms but also in intellectual and spiritual realms. Vivekananda's call for women's independence was a call for them to discover their inner strength and capabilities, thereby contributing more meaningfully to the development of society.

Vivekananda also saw the spiritual strength of women as a crucial component of social reform. He often spoke about the innate spiritual power of women, which could bring compassion, patience, and insight into the societal transformation process. He believed that the qualities typically associated with women, such as empathy and nurturing, were in fact strengths that should be celebrated and utilized in public spheres, including politics and business.

Moreover, Vivekananda's views on women as nation builders

included their participation in politics and governance. He supported women's suffrage and believed that women should have a voice in the laws and policies that affected their lives. By participating in governance, women could ensure that their perspectives and needs were represented, thus leading to more inclusive and effective policies.

Vivekananda's call for the upliftment of women was not limited to any one class or community but was universal. He criticized the harsh conditions under which many women labored, be they rich or poor, and highlighted the importance of improving these conditions for the overall benefit of society. He envisioned a world where women from all backgrounds could achieve their full potential without any barriers.

The idea of women as nation builders also extended to the realm of social reforms. Vivekananda believed that women had a critical role to play in reforming society from within. Whether it was fighting against social evils like child marriage and dowry or advocating for the rights of the underprivileged, women could lead moral and social upliftment movements, thus directly contributing to the building of a stronger nation.

Additionally, Vivekananda emphasized the role of women in preserving and promoting cultural values. He saw women as the custodians of culture and tradition, and he believed that by empowering women, a nation could ensure the preservation of its cultural heritage while also adapting to modernity.

Swami Vivekananda's vision of women as nation builders is a powerful and inspiring aspect of his teachings. He not only recognized the potential of women to contribute to the development of society but actively advocated for their rights and empowerment. His ideas encourage a reevaluation of the role of women in society, urging us to view them not just as participants but as leaders in the collective enterprise of nation-building. By implementing Vivekananda's vision, society can unlock a reservoir of untapped potential that can propel a nation towards greater progress and harmony.

❧❧❧

FIVE

SPIRITUAL FOUNDATIONS FOR DAILY LIVING - INCORPORATING SPIRITUALITY INTO EVERYDAY LIFE

Swami Vivekananda's teachings offer a profound blueprint for integrating spirituality into daily life, presenting it not as an esoteric practice reserved for the few but as accessible and vital to everyone. His ideas on spirituality transcend mere religious practice, suggesting a lifestyle or a way of living that promotes harmony and profound understanding of oneself and the world. This approach to spirituality is particularly resonant today, where the intersection of daily duties and spiritual growth challenges many to find a balance that enriches both aspects of life.

Vivekananda's core message about spirituality was that it should be as natural and necessary as eating or breathing. According to him, spirituality is not about renunciation of the world but about realizing the highest ideals of human existence while actively engaging in the world. He believed that the spiritual foundation of life enhances and does not hinder one's effectiveness in daily activities; rather, it instills a sense of purpose and brings clarity to one's roles and responsibilities.

At the heart of Vivekananda's teaching is the idea that each individual is a manifestation of the divine. Recognizing this divine essence within oneself transforms how one views everyday activities—no longer as mundane tasks but as expressions of divine energy. This shift in perception doesn't require changing what one does, but rather changing how one perceives and approaches these actions. For instance, work, whether in an office or at home, can be seen as worship, as a way to serve humanity and express one's inherent divinity.

Moreover, Vivekananda emphasized the importance of self-control and inner peace as spiritual practices that can be cultivated daily. He taught that mastering one's own mind is essential for leading a spiritual life. This involves practicing concentration and meditation to develop the ability to remain undisturbed by external circumstances and internal emotions. By cultivating such peace, individuals can maintain their spiritual focus amid the hustle and bustle of daily life, making wise decisions that reflect their higher values and aspirations.

Vivekananda also spoke about the power of love and compassion as fundamental spiritual values. He argued that true spirituality manifests through service to others and empathy towards their suffering. Incorporating these values into daily life means approaching relationships and interactions with kindness and understanding, striving to help and uplift others. This approach not only enriches one's own life but also contributes to a more harmonious society.

The practice of seeing the divine in others is another aspect of Vivekananda's spiritual teachings. This practice involves recognizing that everyone, regardless of their social status, religion, or ethnicity, embodies the divine. This recognition can dramatically change interpersonal dynamics, promoting respect and equality and reducing conflict and misunderstanding. It encourages a sense of universal brotherhood and sisterhood, a community where spiritual bonds transcend superficial differences.

Vivekananda's view of integrating spirituality into everyday life also extends to personal development. He advocated for a balanced life that accommodates physical, emotional, and intellectual growth alongside spiritual development. This holistic approach suggests that activities such as physical exercise, intellectual pursuits, and artistic expressions are not separate from spiritual life but are means of expressing and exploring one's spirituality.

Furthermore, Vivekananda stressed the importance of resilience and positive thinking as spiritual tools. He believed that a strong spiritual foundation helps individuals to overcome challenges and setbacks with grace and strength. By maintaining a positive outlook, individuals can transform obstacles into opportunities for growth and learning.

Additionally, the spiritual practice of gratitude plays a crucial role in daily life. Vivekananda taught that recognizing and appreciating the good in one's life, even during tough times, fosters a positive spirit and connects an individual more deeply to their spiritual values. This attitude of gratitude enriches one's life, enhancing feelings of contentment and peace.

Vivekananda's teachings on incorporating spirituality into daily life offer a dynamic and enriching path that does not require withdrawal from the world but rather encourages a deeper engagement with it. By infusing everyday actions with spiritual significance, individuals can lead lives of greater purpose and fulfillment, contributing positively to their communities and the world at large. This approach ensures that spirituality is not confined to specific practices or settings but is woven through the very fabric of daily existence, making life itself a spiritual journey.

SIX

Overcoming Obstacles with Grace - Learning Resilience from Vivekananda's Teachings

Swami Vivekananda's teachings on resilience and overcoming obstacles with grace provide profound insights that are particularly relevant in today's fast-paced and often stressful world. His perspective offers not just strategies but a philosophy of strength and endurance that can empower individuals to face life's challenges with dignity and poise.

Vivekananda's discourse on resilience is anchored in his belief in the infinite potential and inherent strength of every human being. He often emphasized that the true nature of an individual is the soul, which is eternal, unchangeable, and inherently powerful. This core idea forms the foundation of his teachings on overcoming obstacles—by recognizing and tapping into this inner strength, individuals can not only withstand life's trials but can also transcend them.

He often spoke about the importance of self-reliance and mental fortitude. Vivekananda believed that external circumstances could only influence one so far as one allows them to. The real battle, he argued, is waged within the mind. Therefore, mastering one's thoughts and emotions is crucial to developing resilience. He advocated for the practice of meditation and mindfulness as tools to cultivate a focused and steady mind that can remain unshaken in the face of adversity.

Vivekananda's approach to resilience also involves embracing challenges as opportunities for growth. He viewed obstacles not as impediments but as essential elements of the journey toward self-realization and improvement. Each challenge, according to Vivekananda, is a lesson in disguise, meant to strengthen the spirit and build character. This perspective shifts the narrative from one of victimhood to one of empowerment, where every difficulty is a step closer to achieving one's higher self.

Moreover, Vivekananda emphasized the virtue of patience in overcoming obstacles. He argued that many of life's challenges require time and persistence to be resolved or understood. By cultivating patience, individuals can endure difficult times with grace, maintaining their composure and dignity, rather than succumbing to frustration and despair.

Another significant aspect of Vivekananda's teachings on resilience is the power of positive thinking. He believed that thoughts have the power to shape one's reality and that cultivating a positive outlook can significantly alter one's experience of life's challenges. Positive thinking, according to Vivekananda, involves maintaining hope and confidence in the face of difficulties and focusing on solutions rather than problems. This mindset not only alleviates the psychological burden of obstacles but also enhances one's capacity to deal with them effectively.

Vivekananda also stressed the importance of detachment in building resilience. By practicing detachment, individuals can prevent themselves from being overly affected by either success or failure. This equanimity is crucial in maintaining steady progress, regardless of the circumstances. Detachment, as taught by Vivekananda, does not mean disinterest or lack of engagement. Instead, it signifies a deep understanding that the core of one's being is not defined by external successes or failures.

The role of a supportive community and the importance of serving others also play a crucial part in Vivekananda's strategy for overcoming obstacles. He believed that engaging in service not only contributes to the welfare of others but also strengthens the individual's own capacity to handle personal challenges. Service shifts focus from self-centered worries to the needs of others, providing psychological relief and a sense of purpose that can be profoundly empowering in tough times.

Furthermore, Vivekananda encouraged the cultivation of moral strength and integrity as tools for resilience. He taught that sticking to one's principles and maintaining moral discipline can provide the inner strength needed to navigate life's complexities. This integrity ensures that one's actions are aligned with one's values, providing a clear conscience and inner peace that bolster resilience.

Swami Vivekananda's teachings offer a comprehensive guide on overcoming obstacles with grace. By advocating for self-awareness, mental discipline, a positive attitude, patience, detachment, community engagement, and moral integrity, he provides tools that empower individuals to face life's challenges not just with hope and endurance but with confidence and serenity. These teachings not only foster personal growth and resilience but also contribute to the development of a more compassionate and understanding society.

ϷϷϷ

SEVEN

THE VIRTUE OF SERVICE – SELFLESSNESS AND ITS IMPACT ON PERSONAL AND SOCIETAL GROWTH

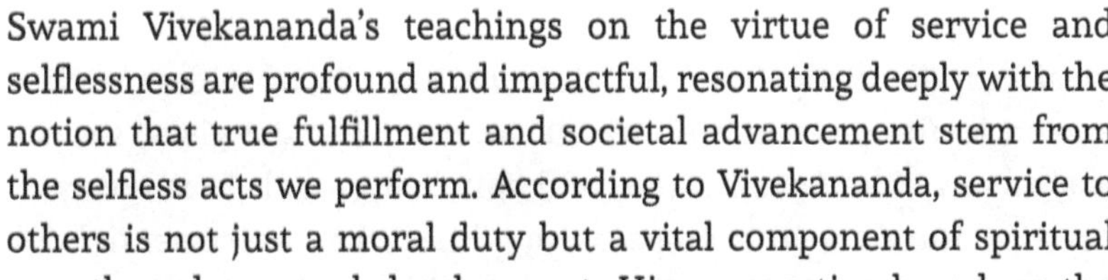

Swami Vivekananda's teachings on the virtue of service and selflessness are profound and impactful, resonating deeply with the notion that true fulfillment and societal advancement stem from the selfless acts we perform. According to Vivekananda, service to others is not just a moral duty but a vital component of spiritual growth and personal development. His perspective broadens the understanding of selflessness, linking it to both personal enlightenment and the broader welfare of society.

Vivekananda placed great emphasis on karma yoga, the path of selfless action, as a means to achieve spiritual growth. He taught that by serving others without expecting anything in return, one purifies the heart and mind, reducing the ego that stands in the way of self-realization. This concept is rooted in the belief that the ego, or the sense of 'I-ness,' is a major barrier to spiritual development. By focusing on the welfare of others, one transcends individual desires and attachments, leading to a state of higher consciousness and inner peace.

The practice of selflessness, as endorsed by Vivekananda, is not merely about performing charitable acts. It involves a profound shift in one's perspective on life and one's role in the world. It means seeing oneself as part of a larger whole and acting in a way that benefits that whole. This shift in perspective encourages individuals to think beyond their personal needs and to act in ways that contribute positively to the community and society at large.

Moreover, Vivekananda's teachings highlight the transformative impact of selfless service on society. He believed that social reform and progress are not achieved solely through policy and governance but also through the individual actions of its citizens. When individuals engage in selfless service, they help create a more compassionate and understanding society. This nurtures a collective spirit and promotes social cohesion, which are essential for addressing the many challenges that societies face.

Vivekananda also pointed out that the benefits of selfless service extend to the giver as well as the receiver. For the giver, service is a means of self-purification and spiritual growth. It is a way to practice humility and empathy, qualities that are essential for personal development. For the receiver, the act of receiving service can provide not only material relief but also emotional and psychological support. Knowing that others care can be a powerful source of comfort and motivation.

Selflessness in service also encourages a sense of responsibility towards the less fortunate and the vulnerable. Vivekananda stressed the importance of serving all without discrimination, reflecting his belief in the underlying unity of all beings. By serving others, individuals affirm the dignity and worth of every human being, thereby fostering an environment of respect and equality.

The practice of selfless service also has practical implications for leadership. Vivekananda taught that true leaders are those who serve their followers rather than command them. This model of leadership, based on empathy, responsibility, and self-sacrifice, can transform management styles and organizational dynamics, leading to more collaborative and supportive work environments.

In addition to its spiritual and social benefits, selfless service contributes to mental health and well-being. Engaging in acts of kindness and helping others can reduce stress, improve emotional well-being, and even enhance physical health. Studies have shown that people who engage in regular volunteer work often experience lower levels of depression, increased life satisfaction, and a greater sense of purpose.

Furthermore, Vivekananda's advocacy for selflessness is particularly relevant in today's globalized world, where individualism often prevails. In a time marked by materialism and competition, the practice of selfless service offers a counter-narrative that promotes shared values and mutual care. It encourages individuals to look beyond their immediate concerns to the needs of the global community, promoting actions that address issues like poverty, inequality, and environmental degradation.

Swami Vivekananda's teachings on the virtue of service and selflessness are a powerful call to action for personal and societal growth. By advocating for a life of service, Vivekananda not only provided a pathway for individual spiritual enlightenment but also laid the groundwork for a more compassionate and cohesive society. The practice of selfless service, according to Vivekananda, is essential for anyone seeking to lead a meaningful life and to contribute positively to the world. His teachings continue to inspire countless individuals to live a life of purpose, guided by the principle of selflessness and the profound impact it can have on the world.

ᗷᗷᗷ

EIGHT

LEADERSHIP INSPIRED BY ETHICS - ETHICAL LEADERSHIP PRINCIPLES FOR MODERN TIMES

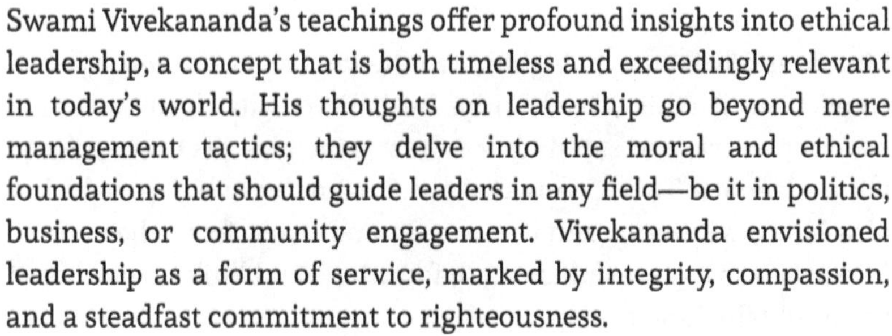

Swami Vivekananda's teachings offer profound insights into ethical leadership, a concept that is both timeless and exceedingly relevant in today's world. His thoughts on leadership go beyond mere management tactics; they delve into the moral and ethical foundations that should guide leaders in any field—be it in politics, business, or community engagement. Vivekananda envisioned leadership as a form of service, marked by integrity, compassion, and a steadfast commitment to righteousness.

At the heart of Vivekananda's philosophy is the principle that true leadership is rooted in moral and ethical purity. He believed that a leader's first duty is to serve others selflessly and to lead by example. This involves demonstrating virtues such as honesty, self-discipline, and a genuine concern for the well-being of others. For Vivekananda, the strength of a leader comes not from their position of power or authority but from their moral character and their ability to inspire trust and respect.

Vivekananda stressed that ethical leadership is based on the idea of universal well-being. He argued that leaders should work towards the greater good, transcending personal and selfish interests. This vision expands the scope of leadership to include the welfare of all humanity, advocating for policies and actions that are inclusive and beneficial to all, not just a select few. This approach challenges leaders to think broadly about the impact of their decisions, considering the long-term effects on society and the environment.

One of the critical aspects of Vivekananda's teachings on leadership is the emphasis on empathy and compassion. He taught that understanding the needs and struggles of others is essential for effective leadership. By putting themselves in the shoes of those they lead, leaders can make more informed and considerate decisions. This empathetic approach fosters a supportive and cooperative environment, encouraging openness and trust within teams and organizations.

Moreover, Vivekananda highlighted the importance of courage and conviction in ethical leadership. He believed that leaders should have the courage to stand up for their principles, even when faced with adversity. This means not only defending what is right but also being willing to admit mistakes and learn from them. Such integrity sets a powerful example for others and builds a culture of accountability and transparency.

Education played a significant role in Vivekananda's concept of leadership. He emphasized that leaders should be well-educated, not just in practical or technical knowledge but in moral philosophy and ethics. Education broadens a leader's perspective and equips them with the tools to solve problems thoughtfully and ethically. Vivekananda advocated for a form of education that fosters critical thinking, self-reflection, and a deep understanding of the interdependence of all life.

Additionally, Vivekananda addressed the need for spiritual development in leadership. He argued that spiritual practices like meditation can help leaders gain clarity, reduce stress, and maintain their focus on ethical principles. The spiritual dimension of leadership according to Vivekananda, involves recognizing a higher purpose in one's actions and being guided by a sense of duty to that purpose.

Vivekananda also spoke about the dangers of ego in leadership. He warned that leaders who are driven by ego and personal gain are likely to misuse their power, leading to corruption and harm. Instead, he promoted the idea of selfless service, where leaders see their role as a duty to serve and uplift others rather than an opportunity to gain power or prestige.

In the context of modern challenges, Vivekananda's teachings on ethical leadership are especially pertinent. In a globalized world, where leaders' decisions can have widespread impacts across international borders, the principles of ethical leadership can guide leaders in navigating complex moral landscapes. Leaders who embrace Vivekananda's ideals can contribute to a more just and sustainable world.

Swami Vivekananda's vision of ethical leadership offers a robust framework for nurturing leaders who are not only effective in achieving their goals but are also committed to the highest ethical standards. His teachings encourage leaders to be moral exemplars, to serve with compassion, and to lead with integrity. By embodying these principles, leaders can inspire real change and make a significant positive impact on the world.

☙☙☙

NINE

HARMONY OF MIND AND BODY – PRACTICES FOR MAINTAINING BALANCE AND HEALTH

Swami Vivekananda placed significant emphasis on the integration and harmony of mind and body, advocating for a balanced approach to health that encompasses both physical well-being and mental clarity. His teachings underline the belief that a healthy mind and a healthy body are interconnected and interdependent, each influencing and sustaining the other. This holistic view of health is crucial, as it addresses the complex interactions between mental and physical states, advocating for practices that promote overall well-being and balance.

Vivekananda's approach to maintaining harmony between mind

and body is rooted in the ancient Indian tradition of Yoga, particularly Raja Yoga, which focuses on controlling the mind through meditation and disciplined practices. He taught that through regular practice of meditation, one can achieve a calm and focused mind, which in turn has a positive effect on physical health. Meditation reduces stress, which is a common cause of numerous physical ailments, including heart disease, hypertension, and immune system disorders. By reducing stress, meditation not only improves mental health but also enhances physical resilience.

Alongside meditation, Vivekananda emphasized the importance of physical exercise and proper diet as essential components of a healthy lifestyle. He was a proponent of the idea that physical fitness was not just for improving bodily health but also for strengthening the mind. Regular physical exercise increases energy levels, improves mood, and boosts overall mental health. Additionally, a well-balanced diet provides the necessary nutrients to fuel both the brain and body, supporting cognitive functions and physical stamina.

Vivekananda also advocated for the practice of Pranayama, or breath control, as a technique for harmonizing the mind and body. Pranayama involves various breathing techniques that help in regulating the life force or 'Prana' within the body. By controlling the breath, one can control the mind, as fluctuations in the mind are often linked to irregularities in breathing. Regular practice of Pranayama enhances lung capacity, improves blood circulation, and stabilizes energy levels, all of which contribute to better physical health and a more balanced mental state.

The concept of self-discipline is another crucial element in Vivekananda's teachings on maintaining health and balance. He believed that self-discipline in habits, thoughts, and actions plays a significant role in achieving harmony between the mind and body. This includes regularity in practices such as meditation and exercise, moderation in diet, and the avoidance of substances that can disrupt physical and mental well-being. Discipline ensures consistency in practices that nurture health, creating a stable foundation for both mental clarity and physical strength.

Vivekananda's perspective on health also encompasses the importance of emotional and psychological well-being. He taught that positive emotions, such as love, compassion, and joy, have a beneficial impact on one's physical health. Conversely, negative emotions, such as anger, fear, and jealousy, can lead to physical problems like digestive issues, heart problems, and decreased immune function. Therefore, cultivating positive emotions through practices like meditation, mindfulness, and acts of kindness is vital for maintaining health and harmony.

Moreover, Vivekananda highlighted the value of sleep in the balance of mind and body. Adequate sleep is essential for cognitive functions and emotional health, as well as for physical repair and recovery. He advocated for a disciplined sleep schedule, suggesting that regular sleep patterns contribute to overall health and well-being.

Vivekananda also recognized the social and environmental factors that influence health. He encouraged individuals to engage in community service and to connect with nature, both of which can have profound effects on mental and physical health. Service to others can provide a sense of purpose and fulfillment, while spending time in nature can reduce stress, enhance mood, and promote physical activity.

Swami Vivekananda's teachings offer a comprehensive framework for achieving harmony between mind and body. Through a combination of physical exercises, dietary habits, mental practices like meditation and Pranayama, emotional cultivation, and a disciplined lifestyle, individuals can maintain balance and health.

This holistic approach not only improves individual well-being but also has the potential to uplift societal health, emphasizing the deep interconnection between personal health and communal harmony.

❦❦❦

TEN

Inner Peace Through Meditation – Simple techniques to start meditating

Inner peace is a state of profound serenity and calm that is largely sought after in today's fast-paced and often chaotic world. Meditation is a powerful tool that has been used for centuries to cultivate this peace and provide deep insights into the workings of the mind and emotions. Swami Vivekananda, a key figure in the introduction of the philosophies of Yoga and Vedanta to the Western world, emphasized meditation as essential for achieving inner peace and spiritual growth. His teachings provide practical guidance on how to begin and sustain a meditation practice, making the profound benefits of meditation accessible to everyone.

Understanding Meditation

Meditation involves training the mind to focus and redirect thoughts. It can increase awareness of oneself and one's surroundings. Practicing meditation can lead to a deeper level of relaxation and a tranquil mind. According to Vivekananda, meditation is not just a practice but a state of being that manifests in calmness, mental clarity, and compassion. To begin meditating, it is crucial to understand its core principles and objectives—primarily, the realization of one's true self beyond the physical and mental planes.

Setting the Environment

The first step in beginning a meditation practice is creating a conducive environment. This space should be quiet, clean, and free from disturbances. Vivekananda suggested that regularity in time and place helps to condition the mind to enter a meditative state more readily. The physical environment can also be enhanced with the presence of soothing elements like soft instrumental music, dim lighting, or incense, which can help in calming the senses and focusing the mind.

Preparing the Mind and Body

Preparation involves physical and mental practices. Physically, one should be comfortable yet alert. Sitting with a straight spine is ideal as it promotes alertness and proper breathing. Vivekananda often emphasized the importance of a stable posture for long periods of meditation. Mentally, preparation involves setting an intention or a resolve that guides the session. This intention could be as simple as seeking calmness or as profound as pursuing self-realization.

Breathing Techniques

Breathing techniques, or Pranayama, are fundamental in meditation as they directly impact the mind's ability to concentrate. Starting with simple techniques like deep abdominal breathing can significantly enhance the ability to meditate. The practice involves slowly inhaling through the nose, allowing the abdomen to expand fully, then exhaling slowly through the nose, ensuring the abdomen contracts completely. This type of breathing helps calm the mind and reduces stress and anxiety, setting a solid foundation for deeper meditation.

Concentration Techniques

Vivekananda taught various concentration techniques to assist in focusing the mind, which is a precursor to deeper meditation. One common method is to focus on a single point or object. This could be a candle flame, a specific sound, or even a mantra. The repetition of a mantra, such as "Om" or any personal or spiritually significant phrase, helps maintain focus and wards off distracting thoughts. As concentration deepens, the mind becomes more stable and ready to transition into meditation.

The Practice of Meditation

The actual practice of meditation begins once the mind has achieved a certain level of concentration. The meditator observes their thoughts and emotions without attachment, letting them pass like clouds in the sky. This practice is sometimes called mindfulness or Vipassana meditation. Another approach, which aligns closely with Vivekananda's teachings, involves delving into deeper states of consciousness, gradually transcending thoughts to experience profound inner peace and silence.

Duration and Regularity

For beginners, Vivekananda recommended short periods of meditation, gradually increasing the duration as one becomes more adept. Starting with as little as five minutes a day and extending to longer periods, regular practice is crucial. Consistency develops the mental discipline needed for meditation and helps to integrate its benefits into everyday life.

Reflection and Integration

After meditation, taking time to gently transition back to normal awareness is important. This might involve some light stretching, walking, or journaling about the experience. Reflecting on the insights gained during meditation can help integrate these learnings into daily life, enhancing overall well-being and inner peace.

Overcoming Challenges

It's normal to encounter obstacles such as restlessness, boredom, or distracting thoughts during meditation. Vivekananda advised patience and persistence in such situations. Returning gently to the focus of the meditation without self-judgment can help overcome these challenges. With regular practice, the frequency and intensity of such disturbances typically diminish.

The Path Forward

Meditation is a journey rather than a destination. As one advances, the insights and experiences deepen, potentially leading to profound personal transformations and a permanent state of peace. Vivekananda's teachings suggest that meditation, when practiced diligently, can unveil the infinite potential within each individual, leading to ultimate freedom and peace.

Through these simple techniques and gradual progression, anyone can start meditating and experience the transformative effects of achieving inner peace, as taught by Swami Vivekananda. This journey not only enriches one's personal life but also enhances one's interactions with others, promoting a deeper sense of empathy, understanding, and compassion. By fostering a calm and mindful approach, individuals can effectively navigate the complexities of modern life, leading to more harmonious relationships and a stronger sense of community.

꩜꩜꩜

ELEVEN

COURAGE IN THE FACE OF ADVERSITY – STORIES OF BRAVERY INSPIRED BY VIVEKANANDA

Swami Vivekananda, a spiritual luminary and a paragon of strength, often spoke about the indispensable quality of courage in the face of adversity. His life and teachings provide numerous examples of bravery that not only inspire but also offer profound insights into how one can harness inner strength to overcome challenges. Vivekananda's messages of fearlessness and resilience are particularly potent in today's context, where individuals and communities face myriad challenges.

Vivekananda's philosophy on courage was deeply influenced by his mentor, Ramakrishna Paramahansa, and rooted in the ancient scriptures of Vedanta, which emphasize the divine nature of the soul and its inherent strength. According to Vivekananda, true courage stems from the realization of one's own spiritual identity and the unshakeable belief that the soul is immortal and beyond harm. This profound understanding instills a kind of bravery that is not merely reactive but a steady, enduring quality that sustains individuals through trials and tribulations.

Vivekananda's Own Journey

The life of Swami Vivekananda himself is a testament to courage in the face of adversity. Born into an aristocratic but financially declining family, Vivekananda faced severe economic hardships from a young age. His quest for spiritual enlightenment led him to Ramakrishna, under whose guidance he embraced a life of spiritual austerity. After the death of his guru, Vivekananda, driven by a profound sense of duty to spread his master's teachings, embarked on a journey across India—a journey fraught with physical hardships and societal skepticism.

Vivekananda's courage shone brightly when he represented Hinduism at the Parliament of the World's Religions in 1893 in Chicago. Despite initial setbacks, including lack of funds and an unknown status, he delivered speeches that not only captivated the audience but also elevated Hindu philosophy on the global stage. His bold assertion of religious tolerance and universal acceptance was a clarion call against the prevailing currents of sectarianism and parochialism.

Stories from Vivekananda's Discourses

Vivekananda often recounted historical and mythical tales to illustrate the virtues of courage and bravery. One such story is that of Prahlada, the boy devotee of Vishnu, who faced the wrath of his father, Hiranyakashipu, for his unshakable devotion. Despite threats and attempts on his life, Prahlada remained steadfast in his faith, embodying the courage that comes from spiritual conviction.

Vivekananda used this story to convey that true bravery does not lie in physical strength but in the power of unyielded spiritual faith.

Another inspiring narrative Vivekananda often cited was that of Jesus Christ, particularly his crucifixion. He highlighted how Christ's life and his ultimate sacrifice were supreme examples of bravery born out of compassion and adherence to one's principles. For Vivekananda, Christ's ability to forgive those who crucified him was the highest form of spiritual bravery, transcending the immediate pain and looking towards a greater good.

Modern Examples Inspired by Vivekananda

Vivekananda's teachings have inspired countless individuals to act courageously in the face of adversity. One notable example is that of freedom fighters in India's struggle for independence. Leaders like Subhas Chandra Bose were deeply influenced by Vivekananda's call for self-sacrifice and service to the nation. Bose's own fearless leadership against the British, despite the risks of imprisonment and death, reflected Vivekananda's ideals of bravery and patriotism.

In contemporary times, Vivekananda's emphasis on courage has motivated individuals across various spheres, from social activists fighting for justice to entrepreneurs overcoming failures to innovate and succeed. His message that inner strength can overcome external circumstances continues to resonate, encouraging people to persist in their endeavors despite setbacks.

The Broader Impact of Courage

Vivekananda believed that individual acts of courage contribute to societal strength and transformation. He maintained that a society that encourages its members to face challenges with courage is more vibrant and resilient. His teachings advocate for a collective spirit where bravery is not just about personal triumph but about uplifting others, fostering a community that can stand strong against adversities.

Swami Vivekananda's teachings on courage are a profound reminder of the power of inner strength and the potential of the human spirit to transcend difficulties. His stories and life serve as a beacon of inspiration, urging us to confront our fears and challenges with a brave heart. Vivekananda's legacy teaches us that it is through bravery in the face of adversity that we can truly evolve both individually and collectively, crafting a narrative of resilience that can stand the test of time. Through his wisdom, Vivekananda continues to inspire courage and hope, showing us that with conviction and faith, no obstacle is insurmountable.

ppp

TWELVE

The Joy of Giving – How generosity enriches our lives

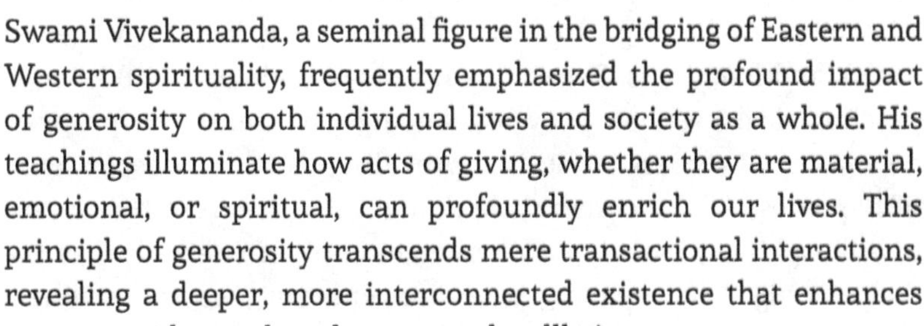

Swami Vivekananda, a seminal figure in the bridging of Eastern and Western spirituality, frequently emphasized the profound impact of generosity on both individual lives and society as a whole. His teachings illuminate how acts of giving, whether they are material, emotional, or spiritual, can profoundly enrich our lives. This principle of generosity transcends mere transactional interactions, revealing a deeper, more interconnected existence that enhances our personal growth and communal wellbeing.

The Essence of Generosity

Generosity, according to Vivekananda, is not confined to the donation of material goods or money, but encompasses a broader spectrum of giving that includes sharing knowledge, offering emotional support, and extending kindness to others. This expansive view of generosity is rooted in the belief that true joy comes from serving others without expecting anything in return. Vivekananda posited that the act of giving itself is the reward, aligning closely with the concept of Karma Yoga, the path of selfless action.

Generosity as a Path to Self-Realization

Vivekananda often spoke about self-realization as the ultimate goal of human life, and he saw generosity as a vital means to achieve this state. By giving selflessly, we diminish the ego, which is often a barrier to recognizing our true self — our spiritual nature. Every act of giving, therefore, serves as a practice of reducing our self-centered tendencies, helping us to realize that we are part of a larger, interconnected universe. This realization fosters a sense of unity and empathy with others, deepening our spiritual journey.

The Psychological Benefits of Giving

Modern psychology supports Vivekananda's views on the benefits of generosity, linking altruistic behavior with increased mental health and happiness. Research suggests that giving can boost our psychological wellbeing by enhancing our sense of purpose, decreasing our stress levels, and providing us with a deeper sense of happiness. These benefits are thought to arise from the release of endorphins, producing a phenomenon often referred to as the "helper's high." By engaging in acts of generosity, we not only help others but also cultivate our own mental and emotional health.

Generosity and Community Building

Vivekananda emphasized the importance of generosity in strengthening communities. He believed that when individuals act generously, they lay the foundations for trust and cooperation, which are essential for any thriving community. Generosity promotes social connection by breaking down barriers between people, fostering an environment where individuals can unite for common causes. This collective strength is crucial for addressing broader societal issues such as poverty, inequality, and injustice.

The Ripple Effects of Generosity

One of the most powerful aspects of generosity is its potential to inspire further acts of kindness. Vivekananda highlighted that every act of generosity can set off a chain reaction, encouraging recipients and onlookers alike to engage in their own acts of giving. This multiplier effect can exponentially increase the positive impact of a single generous act, spreading goodwill far beyond the initial interaction.

Challenges and Considerations in Practicing Generosity

While advocating for generosity, Vivekananda also acknowledged the challenges that come with it. One such challenge is the potential for dependency, where recipients may become reliant on external help. Vivekananda advised that generosity should empower rather than disable, suggesting that we should aim to help others become self-reliant rather than continually dependent.

Furthermore, Vivekananda warned against performative generosity, where acts of giving are done for personal gain or recognition rather than genuine concern. True generosity, he argued, is marked by humility and the absence of pride or ego, emphasizing the purity of intention in the act of giving.

Generosity in Everyday Life

Implementing Vivekananda's teachings on generosity involves integrating small acts of kindness into our daily lives. This could be as simple as offering a genuine compliment, spending time with someone who needs company, or sharing a skill with others without expecting payment. Each act, no matter how small, contributes to a greater culture of generosity.

Swami Vivekananda's teachings on the joy of giving offer profound insights into how generosity enriches our lives. By embracing a generous spirit, we not only enhance our own lives but also contribute to the welfare of our communities and society at large. Generosity, as Vivekananda teaches, is a key to unlocking deeper spiritual understanding, fostering psychological wellbeing, and building stronger communities. Through the simple yet powerful act of giving, we discover the interconnectedness of life and the true joy that comes from serving others.

ÞÞÞ

THIRTEEN

FOSTERING COMMUNITY SPIRIT – BUILDING SUPPORTIVE NETWORKS FOR EMPOWERMENT."

Swami Vivekananda, a visionary who significantly influenced the conceptual framework of community and individual empowerment, emphasized the profound importance of fostering community spirit. His teachings encourage the creation of supportive networks that empower individuals and strengthen communal bonds. According to Vivekananda, a true community is not just a collection of individuals but a dynamic, integrated entity where each member actively contributes to and benefits from the collective well-being.

The Concept of Collective Empowerment

Vivekananda's idea of collective empowerment is rooted in the belief that the strength of a community lies in its unity and the active participation of its members. He saw community as a platform for mutual growth, where the spiritual, emotional, and material well-being of each person is interlinked with that of others. This holistic approach underlines that individual progress and community development are not mutually exclusive but are deeply interconnected.

Spiritual Foundation of Community

One of the cornerstone teachings of Vivekananda about community building is the spiritual foundation it requires. He argued that spirituality should not be confined to individual practice but should extend to the way communities function. Spirituality, in this context, involves seeing beyond one's selfish interests, recognizing the divine in every individual, and striving for the common good.

This perspective fosters a sense of respect, empathy, and unconditional support among community members, crucial for building strong, sustainable networks.

Role of Education in Empowerment

Vivekananda placed immense importance on education as a tool for empowerment. He advocated for an education system that goes beyond academic learning to include moral and ethical teachings, which prepare individuals not only for personal success but also for active and responsible participation in their communities.

Education, according to Vivekananda, should cultivate a sense of duty towards one's community and inspire individuals to contribute positively. This approach ensures that education becomes a means of empowering individuals to act as agents of change within their networks.

Community Service as a Unifying Force

Community service is another significant theme in Vivekananda's teachings on fostering community spirit. He believed that selfless service is one of the most powerful means to unite people from different backgrounds. Engaging in community service projects allows individuals to work towards a common goal, building a sense of camaraderie and mutual trust. Moreover, service projects help highlight and address the community's needs, ensuring that the efforts of its members are directed towards tangible, beneficial outcomes.

Overcoming Barriers Through Inclusivity

Vivekananda was a strong proponent of inclusivity and diversity within community settings. He emphasized that a community's strength is enhanced by the diversity of its members, provided that this diversity is embraced with openness and respect.

Building supportive networks, therefore, involves creating inclusive spaces that respect and celebrate differences. This inclusivity ensures that all members feel valued and empowered to share their unique perspectives and skills, enriching the community as a whole.

Communication as the Lifeline of Community

Effective communication is crucial for fostering community spirit, as it ensures transparency, facilitates understanding, and resolves conflicts. Vivekananda highlighted the importance of honest and open communication in building and maintaining trust within the community.

Regular interactions, community meetings, and open forums encourage members to express their views and contribute to decision-making processes, enhancing their investment in community initiatives.

Leadership in Community Building

Leadership plays a pivotal role in community spirit and empowerment. Vivekananda described true leaders as those who serve with humility and lead by example. Effective community leaders are those who inspire by their actions, encourage participation from all members, and prioritize the community's welfare over personal agendas. Such leadership cultivates a supportive environment where members feel motivated and empowered to take initiative and contribute to the community's objectives.

Sustainability Through Shared Values

For a community to be sustainable, it must be anchored in shared values and goals. Vivekananda encouraged communities to collectively identify and commit to core values such as mutual respect, cooperation, and the pursuit of common goals. These shared values become the guiding principles that drive the community's efforts and ensure that the network remains resilient in the face of challenges.

In essence, fostering community spirit as envisioned by Swami Vivekananda involves building networks that not only support and empower individuals but also create a collective force capable of societal transformation. Through spirituality, education, service, inclusivity, effective communication, inspirational leadership, and shared values, communities can develop strong bonds and a robust support system.

These networks, in turn, empower each member, leading to a more harmonious, productive, and fulfilling collective existence. By nurturing such environments, we pave the way for a society where empowerment is not an individual struggle but a communal achievement.

ϷϷϷ

FOURTEEN

MINDFULNESS IN MODERN TIMES – STAYING PRESENT AND MINDFUL IN A BUSY WORLD

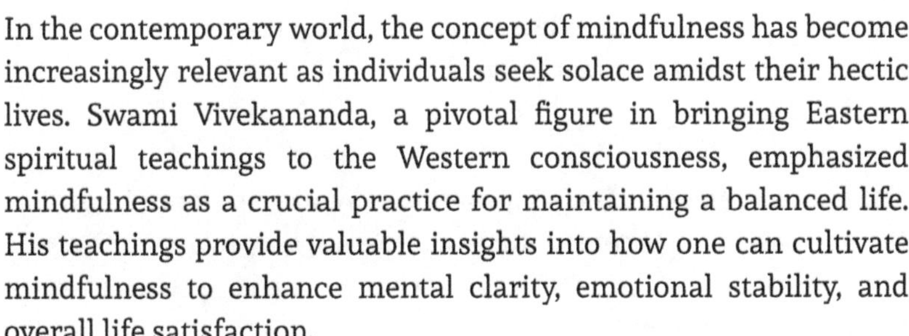

In the contemporary world, the concept of mindfulness has become increasingly relevant as individuals seek solace amidst their hectic lives. Swami Vivekananda, a pivotal figure in bringing Eastern spiritual teachings to the Western consciousness, emphasized mindfulness as a crucial practice for maintaining a balanced life. His teachings provide valuable insights into how one can cultivate mindfulness to enhance mental clarity, emotional stability, and overall life satisfaction.

Mindfulness, as discussed by Vivekananda, involves a conscious awareness of our present moment—being fully aware of what we are doing and how we are feeling without being overly reactive or overwhelmed by what's happening around us. This practice is rooted in ancient philosophic traditions that see the control of the mind as a key to personal growth and enlightenment. In modern times, mindfulness has been recognized for its benefits in stress reduction, mental health, and overall well-being.

Vivekananda's advocacy for mindfulness is deeply embedded in the Yogic traditions, particularly the Yoga Sutras of Patanjali, which emphasize the importance of controlling the mind as a means to achieve spiritual awakening. These teachings suggest that through mindfulness, individuals can detach from their automatic thoughts and reactions, which often lead to stress and emotional turmoil.

The practical benefits of mindfulness in contemporary society are manifold. Scientific research supports that regular mindfulness practice improves concentration, enhances cognitive flexibility, reduces symptoms of anxiety and depression, and boosts overall emotional resilience. Furthermore, mindfulness has been shown to improve physical health by lowering blood pressure, reducing chronic pain, and enhancing sleep.

Vivekananda proposed several practical ways to integrate mindfulness into daily life, advocating for its practice not only during formal meditation but also throughout the day. He suggested that mindfulness can be cultivated through simple practices such as:

Conscious Breathing: Focusing on one's breath, a practice known as Pranayama in Yogic terms, is a fundamental way to anchor oneself in the present moment. This practice can be used anytime to return to the present and reduce stress.

Mindful Eating: Vivekananda encouraged being fully present while eating, appreciating the flavors and textures of food, and being aware of the act of nourishment, which can transform a routine activity into a profound practice of mindfulness.

Engaged Listening: Mindfulness can be practiced through active and engaged listening, which involves fully concentrating on what is being said without planning the next thing to say or being distracted by external thoughts.

One of the challenges of practicing mindfulness in modern times is the constant barrage of distractions from technology and other sources. Vivekananda emphasized the importance of regular meditation to strengthen the mind's ability to focus and resist distractions. He recommended setting aside specific times for meditation and gradually increasing these periods, training the mind to remain present despite external stimuli.

In the realm of work, Vivekananda saw mindfulness as essential for maintaining productivity and creativity. He believed that a mindful approach to work, where one is fully immersed in the tasks at hand, can transform mundane activities into spiritually uplifting experiences. This approach not only enhances job performance but also contributes to personal and professional fulfillment.

Vivekananda stressed that mindfulness should extend to interactions with others, promoting compassion and empathy. By being present in our interactions, we are better able to connect with others on a deeper level, improving our relationships and fostering a more compassionate community.

The long-term practice of mindfulness leads to what Vivekananda described as an "expansion of the self." This expansion involves moving beyond narrow self-interest to a wider perspective that includes the well-being of others. This shift is crucial for personal development and is a cornerstone of spiritual growth.

Swami Vivekananda's insights into mindfulness offer a timeless wisdom that is profoundly relevant in today's fast-paced world. By practicing mindfulness, individuals can manage stress, improve their health, and experience deeper levels of peace and satisfaction. Moreover, mindfulness fosters a greater connection to others and the world around us, contributing to a more harmonious and compassionate society. Embracing these practices allows individuals to navigate the complexities of modern life with grace and wisdom, staying present and mindful amidst the busyness of everyday existence.

ÞÞÞ

FIFTEEN

RESPECTING NATURE'S WISDOM - ENVIRONMENTAL CONSCIOUSNESS AS A SPIRITUAL PRACTICE

In an era marked by profound environmental challenges, the teachings of Swami Vivekananda on respecting nature's wisdom offer timeless insights into the interdependence of spiritual practice and environmental consciousness. Vivekananda, a visionary spiritual leader, emphasized that the reverence for nature is not only an ethical imperative but also a vital component of spiritual growth. His views can guide us in cultivating a deeper environmental consciousness, fostering a harmonious relationship between humanity and the natural world.

Vivekananda viewed nature as a manifestation of the divine,

teaching that everything in the universe is imbued with spiritual significance. This perspective invites a profound respect for the natural world, encouraging individuals to see nature not as a resource to be exploited, but as a sacred entity to be revered and protected. According to Vivekananda, true spiritual practice involves recognizing the divine in all forms of life, which naturally leads to actions that respect and preserve the environment.

For Vivekananda, environmental consciousness was an integral part of spiritual development. He advocated for a lifestyle that respects ecological balance and conserves nature's resources. This approach involves more than just reducing one's ecological footprint—it includes developing a mindfulness of how everyday actions impact the natural world. Vivekananda encouraged his followers to consider the environmental consequences of their choices in food, consumption, and even travel, promoting a way of life that is in harmony with the planet.

Vivekananda's teachings on karma—actions and their consequences—also extend to the environmental context. He posited that just as our actions towards others return to us, so too do our actions towards the environment. This karmic perspective underscores the importance of treating nature with respect and care, as the degradation we contribute to can come back to affect us in the form of environmental crises. Thus, environmental responsibility is seen not just as a duty but as a necessary aspect of spiritual and ethical living.

Vivekananda emphasized practical measures that individuals and communities can adopt to enhance their environmental consciousness. These include:

Sustainable Living: Advocating for a lifestyle that minimizes waste and maximizes the reuse and recycling of resources. This includes choosing sustainable products, reducing energy consumption, and supporting eco-friendly technologies.

Plant-based Diet: Promoting a diet that respects animal life and has a lower environmental impact. Vivekananda highlighted the benefits of vegetarianism, which not only aligns with non-harming principles (ahimsa) but also contributes less to environmental degradation compared to meat-based diets.

Conservation Efforts: Encouraging active participation in conservation efforts, whether by planting trees, cleaning up natural sites, or supporting policies and initiatives that protect the environment.

Education and Advocacy: Spreading awareness about the importance of environmental conservation through education and advocacy. Vivekananda believed in the power of informed communities to enact change, emphasizing the role of education in fostering a deeper connection with nature.

Vivekananda placed a strong emphasis on the power of community in effecting environmental change. He envisioned communities that work together to protect and preserve their natural surroundings, recognizing that collective efforts are often more effective. Community gardens, cooperative conservation projects, and local sustainability initiatives are all examples of how communal efforts can lead to significant environmental benefits.

Vivekananda often spoke of nature as a source of spiritual inspiration and renewal. He encouraged spending time in nature to not only appreciate its beauty but to draw spiritual strength from it. This practice helps to foster a personal connection with the environment, making the protection of nature a more heartfelt commitment rather than a mere moral duty.

Swami Vivekananda's teachings on respecting nature's wisdom

illuminate the deep connection between environmental health and spiritual well-being. By adopting a lifestyle that respects and protects the natural world, we engage in a form of spiritual practice that honors the divine in all its forms. This holistic approach not only contributes to personal growth but also addresses some of the most pressing environmental issues of our time. As we become more conscious of the impact of our actions on the planet, we can follow in Vivekananda's footsteps, embracing environmental consciousness as a core element of our spiritual practice. This integration of spirituality and environmentalism can lead us towards a more sustainable, just, and harmonious world.

ᗞᗞᗞ

SIXTEEN

THE ART OF COMMUNICATION - EFFECTIVE WAYS TO CONVEY THOUGHTS AND EMOTIONS

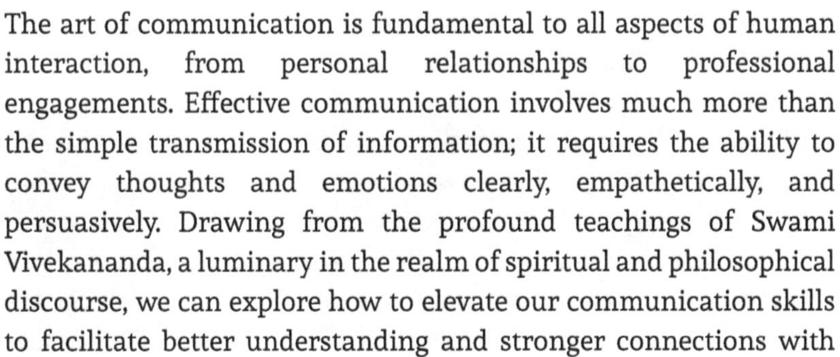

The art of communication is fundamental to all aspects of human interaction, from personal relationships to professional engagements. Effective communication involves much more than the simple transmission of information; it requires the ability to convey thoughts and emotions clearly, empathetically, and persuasively. Drawing from the profound teachings of Swami Vivekananda, a luminary in the realm of spiritual and philosophical discourse, we can explore how to elevate our communication skills to facilitate better understanding and stronger connections with others.

Effective communication hinges on clarity, empathy, authenticity, and responsiveness. These components ensure that messages are not only delivered but also received and understood as intended. Vivekananda, known for his eloquent speeches and deep insights, demonstrated these qualities in his interactions. He emphasized the importance of clarity of thought and precision in expression, advocating that one should speak only what one truly understands and believes.

Vivekananda often noted that simplicity is key to clarity. He advised that when conveying ideas, especially complex or profound ones, one should use simple language. Simplifying your language does not mean diluting your message but rather making it accessible to a broader audience. This approach ensures that the essence of the message is not lost in translation and that the audience can engage with the content effectively.

Empathy in communication involves a deep understanding of the audience's perspectives, feelings, and contexts. Vivekananda demonstrated this through his tailored speeches across different cultures and contexts, always aiming to connect with his audience on an emotional level. He believed that to communicate effectively, one must listen intently and empathetically, responding to the audience's emotional and intellectual needs. This reciprocal understanding not only enhances the communication process but also builds trust and rapport.

Authenticity in communication builds trust and credibility. Vivekananda conveyed his messages with a heartfelt sincerity that resonated deeply with his listeners. He taught that one's words should reflect one's true beliefs and values. Honesty in communication fosters transparency and openness, which are crucial for meaningful interactions. It allows for genuine connections to be formed and facilitates the open exchange of ideas and feelings.

Effective communication is inherently interactive. It involves not only speaking but also listening, not only informing but also understanding. Vivekananda engaged with his audience by asking questions, seeking feedback, and reflecting on responses. This dynamic approach ensures that communication is a two-way process, allowing for adjustments and improvements in real-time, based on how the message is received and interpreted.

Vivekananda also highlighted the importance of nonverbal cues in communication. Body language, eye contact, facial expressions, and tone of voice play significant roles in conveying emotions and intentions. He was known for his commanding presence and the ability to capture attention through his poise and sincerity. Effective communicators are aware of their nonverbal signals and how they complement or contradict their words, adjusting them to ensure consistency and enhance the message.

Understanding the context is critical for effective communication. This includes the cultural, social, and emotional contexts in which communication occurs. Vivekananda adapted his messages according to the cultural norms and expectations of his audiences, which varied widely as he traveled across the world. Being sensitive to the context can prevent misunderstandings and foster a more inclusive and respectful communication environment.

Vivekananda believed in the continuous improvement of oneself, including one's communication skills. He advocated for regular self-reflection and learning from each interaction. Effective communicators continually refine their skills, learn from their experiences, and adapt to new challenges and environments. This growth mindset not only improves individual communication skills but also enhances the overall quality of interactions within a community or organization.

The art of communication as taught by Swami Vivekananda

encompasses a variety of skills and attributes, including clarity, empathy, authenticity, responsiveness, and an understanding of nonverbal cues and context. By embracing these principles, individuals can enhance their ability to effectively convey thoughts and emotions, leading to better personal and professional relationships. Communication is not just about exchanging information; it's about connecting with others, understanding diverse perspectives, and building communities based on mutual respect and understanding. In embracing Vivekananda's teachings, we can aspire to not only become better communicators but also more compassionate and connected individuals in a complex world.

ÞÞÞ

SEVENTEEN

CULTIVATING POSITIVE RELATIONSHIPS - TIPS FOR NURTURING HEALTHY INTERPERSONAL CONNECTIONS

Cultivating positive relationships is an essential aspect of a fulfilling life. Relationships, whether familial, romantic, professional, or social, provide support, joy, and enrichment. However, nurturing these connections requires thoughtful effort, understanding, and genuine care. The teachings of Swami Vivekananda, a spiritual leader renowned for his profound wisdom on human nature and interpersonal dynamics, offer valuable insights into developing and maintaining healthy relationships.

At the core of all healthy relationships is a foundation of trust and respect. Vivekananda emphasized the importance of these qualities, teaching that respect for others stems from recognizing their inherent worth and treating them with dignity, regardless of their circumstances or behavior. Trust, on the other hand, is built through consistency in words and actions. Vivekananda advocated for honesty and integrity as the pillars of trust. By consistently being reliable and truthful, individuals can foster a sense of security and confidence in their relationships.

Empathy is the ability to understand and share the feelings of another. Vivekananda highlighted empathy as crucial for nurturing relationships because it allows individuals to connect with others on a deeper level. Practicing empathy involves listening actively and without judgment, trying to see situations from the other person's perspective, and responding with compassion and sensitivity. This empathetic engagement helps in resolving conflicts, providing support, and strengthening bonds.

Effective communication is indispensable in building and maintaining healthy relationships. Vivekananda taught that clear, honest, and kind communication is necessary to avoid misunderstandings and build a stronger rapport. He advised that individuals should listen more than they speak and when they do speak, it should be with thoughtfulness and care. Additionally, nonverbal cues such as body language, eye contact, and facial expressions should align with verbal messages to convey sincerity and attentiveness.

Vivekananda believed in the power of uplifting others. In any relationship, the mutual exchange of support and encouragement plays a significant role in its health and longevity. Supporting each other's goals, offering encouragement during challenging times, and celebrating successes together can greatly enhance the bond between individuals. This supportive dynamic not only fosters personal growth but also solidifies the relationship as a source of positive reinforcement and mutual inspiration.

Vivekananda spoke often about the virtue of forgiveness, emphasizing its importance in healing and sustaining relationships. Holding onto grudges or dwelling on past conflicts can erode trust and affection, whereas forgiveness can restore harmony. Alongside forgiveness, flexibility in expectations and the willingness to adapt are crucial. Recognizing that people change and situations evolve helps in maintaining realistic expectations and contributes to the resilience of the relationship.

While differences can enrich relationships, shared values and interests provide a common ground that can strengthen interpersonal connections. Vivekananda encouraged individuals to explore and engage in activities that both parties value or enjoy. This not only provides opportunities for enjoyable and meaningful experiences together but also reinforces the compatibility and companionship that are essential for a lasting relationship.

Vivekananda underscored the importance of personal growth and independence within relationships. A healthy relationship allows individuals to grow independently, pursue their interests, and fulfill their potential, without feeling restrained by the relationship. Encouraging and respecting each other's need for personal space and individual pursuits enhances mutual respect and reduces the pressures that can arise from excessive dependency.

Finally, Vivekananda advocated for continuous improvement in oneself and one's relationships. He believed that just as individuals evolve, so too should relationships. Regular reflection on how to better support and connect with each other can keep the relationship dynamic and responsive to the needs of both parties.

In essence, cultivating positive relationships according to Swami Vivekananda's teachings involves building trust and respect, practicing empathy, communicating effectively, offering mutual support, embracing forgiveness and flexibility, sharing values, encouraging independence, and committing to continuous improvement. These principles foster not only healthier and more fulfilling relationships but also contribute to a richer, more compassionate life. By integrating these timeless teachings into daily interactions, individuals can nurture and sustain the kind of relationships that provide joy, support, and profound connection.

ဗဗဗ

EIGHTEEN

EMPOWERMENT THROUGH ENTREPRENEURSHIP – ENCOURAGING WOMEN TO EXPLORE BUSINESS VENTURES

Empowerment through entrepreneurship represents a pivotal avenue for enabling women to achieve economic independence, build self-confidence, and effect societal change. The realm of entrepreneurship offers unique opportunities for women to assert their creativity, leadership, and decision-making skills, fostering not only personal growth but also contributing to the broader economic and social fabric. Drawing on the principles of empowerment and self-reliance advocated by visionary leaders like Swami Vivekananda, this narrative explores the multifaceted benefits of encouraging women to embark on entrepreneurial ventures.

Economic independence is fundamental to personal empowerment. For many women, entrepreneurship provides a path to achieve financial autonomy, which in turn enhances their ability to make choices about their lives, from education to health to living conditions. Swami Vivekananda emphasized the significance of self-reliance, and in the context of women's entrepreneurship, this translates into the ability to generate one's own income, which is a crucial step towards breaking free from dependence and societal constraints.

Entrepreneurship serves as a powerful tool for women to challenge and break through societal barriers that often confine them to traditional roles. By stepping into roles of business ownership and leadership, women not only challenge the stereotypical gender roles but also set a precedent for others. Each successful woman entrepreneur becomes a role model and a beacon of possibility for other women, especially in cultures where women's economic roles have traditionally been limited.

Entrepreneurship inherently involves innovation and creativity. For women, the entrepreneurial journey offers a platform to express their creativity, pursue their passions, and implement innovative solutions to problems. Women bring unique perspectives to business, often driving them towards ventures that are community-oriented, socially responsible, and innovative. Their approach can lead to the development of products and services that cater more effectively to market needs, often overlooked by mainstream businesses.

Running a business requires a wide range of skills from financial management to strategic planning to customer relations. As women entrepreneurs grow their businesses, they also build essential skills and confidence in their abilities. Leadership is particularly crucial; as women lead teams, make decisions, and navigate challenges, they develop a robust sense of self-efficacy. This growth in confidence and skills has ripple effects, enhancing their roles within families and communities and fostering a culture of leadership among other women.

Women's entrepreneurship is not just beneficial on an individual level; it also contributes significantly to broader economic growth. Businesses led by women tend to reinvest a considerable portion of their earnings into their families and communities, leading to better education, health, and overall economic conditions. Additionally, by increasing women's participation in the economy, new job opportunities are created, which further stimulates economic activity and development.

Entrepreneurship can be a challenging journey, making the availability of supportive networks crucial. These networks provide mentorship, advice, financial resources, and emotional support. For women, who may face greater obstacles in accessing resources and networks, establishing strong support systems is even more crucial. Initiatives aimed at building networks for women entrepreneurs can facilitate the sharing of knowledge and resources, helping to overcome barriers to market entry and business growth.

For women's entrepreneurship to thrive, supportive policies and institutional frameworks are essential. This includes access to finance, education and training in business skills, legal support, and protection against discriminatory practices. Governments and organizations can play a significant role in providing these supports through targeted programs that address the specific needs of women entrepreneurs.

Women entrepreneurs often drive social innovation by addressing community-specific problems through their businesses. Whether it's through products that improve health and well-being, services that enhance access to education, or innovations that protect the environment, women-led enterprises frequently embed social goals in their business models, thereby contributing to sustainable community development.

Encouraging women to explore entrepreneurship not only empowers them individually but also has profound implications for societal and economic development. As Swami Vivekananda's teachings suggest, fostering self-reliance and courage among women through entrepreneurship can lead to transformative outcomes. It nurtures a culture where women are valued not only for their economic contributions but also for their role in leading and inspiring change. In promoting women's entrepreneurship, society can progress towards greater equality, innovation, and economic resilience, reflecting a true empowerment paradigm.

ᐅᐅᐅ

NINETEEN

LEGACY OF KINDNESS - VIVEKANANDA'S TEACHINGS ON BEING KIND IN A COMPETITIVE WORLD

In a world often driven by competition and individualism, the teachings of Swami Vivekananda stand out as a beacon of kindness and compassion. Vivekananda, a revered spiritual leader and philosopher, emphasized that true success and fulfillment come from selflessness and the sincere wish to benefit others. His perspective offers profound insights into how individuals can cultivate kindness in a competitive environment, encouraging a legacy that transcends personal achievements to include the welfare of others.

At the heart of Vivekananda's teachings is the principle of selflessness. He believed that the essence of all religions and spiritual pursuits is to serve and to give selflessly. Kindness, according to Vivekananda, is not merely an ethical duty but a fundamental aspect of one's spiritual identity. By practicing kindness, individuals can connect with their deeper selves, which Vivekananda identified as inherently pure and altruistic.

Vivekananda recognized that competition is a natural part of human life, particularly in the socio-economic spheres. However, he argued that competition should not breed hostility, envy, or greed. Instead, it should be viewed as a pathway to excellence where the focus is on self-improvement and the betterment of one's capabilities, rather than surpassing others at any cost. Vivekananda's teachings encourage viewing competitors as comrades in the journey of growth, fostering a spirit of mutual respect and kindness.

Vivekananda posited that kindness enriches the giver as much as, if not more than, the receiver. Acts of kindness, he argued, refine one's character and elevate one's consciousness. They diminish ego and broaden one's perspective, leading to greater emotional maturity and inner peace. Moreover, kindness in interactions creates positive feedback loops; it encourages others to act kindly, thereby fostering an environment where cooperative and supportive relationships thrive.

In the competitive world of business and leadership, kindness is often underestimated. Yet, Vivekananda championed the idea that true leaders are those who serve their followers with kindness and empathy. He believed that leadership grounded in compassion is more sustainable and effective. Leaders who demonstrate kindness foster loyalty, encourage open communication, and inspire their teams to commit wholeheartedly to shared goals.

Vivekananda suggested practical ways to cultivate kindness daily, even in competitive settings:

Empathy: Make a conscious effort to understand and empathize with others' feelings and viewpoints. This can transform competition into a drive for mutual success.

Mentorship: Share knowledge and experience generously. Guiding others in their professional journey not only aids their development but also enriches the mentor's sense of purpose.

Fair Play: Commit to fairness and integrity in all dealings. Recognize that winning at the expense of others' dignity or rights is a hollow victory.

Support Others' Success: Celebrate the achievements of peers and competitors. Such generosity of spirit is often reciprocated and leads to stronger, more respectful relationships.

Volunteerism: Engage in community service or social work. These activities provide a broader perspective on the impact of kindness.

Vivekananda stressed that kindness should permeate all aspects of life, not just personal interactions. He advocated for policies and practices in business and governance that prioritize the welfare of all stakeholders, including employees, communities, and the environment. In a competitive world, such policies may seem counterintuitive, but they are essential for creating sustainable systems that benefit society as a whole.

The legacy of kindness, as envisioned by Vivekananda, is a continuous chain of positive actions inspired by each act of kindness. He believed that every individual has the potential to spark change in their immediate environment, which can ripple outwards to transform larger communities and, eventually, the world.

Swami Vivekananda's teachings on kindness offer a powerful counter-narrative to the often cutthroat nature of competitive environments. By integrating kindness into our daily lives and institutional frameworks, we not only enhance our personal and spiritual growth but also contribute to a more compassionate and equitable world. Kindness, therefore, is not just a moral virtue but a practical and transformative strategy for personal and collective success in a competitive world.

TWENTY

Swami Vivekananda, a profound philosopher and spiritual leader, espoused ideals that not only bridged the spiritual and the secular but also advocated for the empowerment of women. His vision for the future was clear—empower women to become leaders who can shape and influence society with strength and compassion. This essay explores how Vivekananda's teachings can inspire a new generation of women leaders, equipping them with the philosophical and practical tools to lead with integrity and vision.

Vivekananda placed great emphasis on the education and empowerment of women. He believed that a nation's progress was not possible without the active participation of women. He famously said, "The best thermometer to the progress of a nation is its treatment of its women." By advocating for women's education, Vivekananda laid the groundwork for creating leaders who are not only skilled and knowledgeable but also morally and ethically strong.

According to Vivekananda, education is the primary means through which women can gain the freedom to express and become agents of change in society. He stressed that education should not be limited to academic knowledge but should also include spiritual and moral education, which cultivates the inner strength necessary to face life's challenges. For the new generation of women leaders, this holistic approach to education enables them to harness their full potential and lead with a balance of wisdom and compassion.

Vivekananda's teachings on spiritual empowerment emphasize understanding one's deeper purpose and connection to a larger reality. He encouraged individuals to realize their own divinity and use it as a source of strength. For women, this spiritual empowerment can be particularly transformative, providing a firm anchor in the often tumultuous landscape of leadership roles. It instills a sense of purpose that transcends societal expectations and personal ambition, orienting women leaders towards service and societal welfare.

Drawing from the concept of Karma Yoga, or the yoga of selfless action, Vivekananda redefined leadership as service. He believed that true leaders are those who serve with humility and work for the well-being of others without seeking personal gain. This approach to leadership can profoundly influence how women leaders shape their strategies and decision-making processes. It promotes a leadership style that is inclusive, empathetic, and focused on the common good.

Vivekananda recognized that women often face significant barriers, both societal and self-imposed, that hinder their progress. He advocated for women to cultivate self-confidence and assertiveness as tools to overcome these barriers. By internalizing Vivekananda's teachings on strength and perseverance, women can navigate challenges more effectively and assert their rightful place in leadership roles.

Integrity and ethics were central to Vivekananda's teachings. He urged leaders to adhere to the highest standards of honesty and moral righteousness. For the new generation of women leaders, maintaining ethical integrity is crucial not only for personal credibility but also for inspiring trust and loyalty among followers. Ethical leadership also ensures that the pursuit of goals and objectives does not compromise moral values but instead uplifts society.

Vivekananda highlighted the importance of community and support networks in fostering individual and collective growth. For women leaders, building and maintaining supportive networks can be instrumental. These networks provide mentorship, encouragement, and resources that are essential for navigating the complexities of leadership. They also serve as platforms for sharing knowledge and experiences, which can empower more women to step into leadership roles.

Vivekananda urged individuals to cultivate a visionary outlook, which involves looking beyond the immediate and material to envision a better future. For women leaders, developing a visionary perspective means setting transformative goals that seek to improve not just their organizations but also society at large. This kind of foresight is crucial for addressing complex global challenges and for driving sustainable development.

Swami Vivekananda's ideals provide a rich and empowering framework for inspiring a new generation of women leaders. His emphasis on education, spiritual empowerment, service, integrity, and visionary leadership offers valuable guidance for women aiming to lead with impact and compassion. By embodying these principles, women leaders can not only achieve professional success but also contribute to creating a more just and equitable world. Vivekananda's vision for the future, therefore, not only uplifts women but also enriches the entire fabric of leadership and community life.

ᐅᐅᐅ

TWENTY-ONE
SUMMARY

Swami Vivekananda's teachings provide a comprehensive guide to personal and social development, offering timeless wisdom that can be applied to various aspects of modern life—from personal ethics to leadership and community engagement. This summary chapter encapsulates the core themes explored through Vivekananda's teachings and illustrates how they can inspire and guide individuals today in cultivating a fulfilling, balanced, and impactful life.

1. The Power of Self-Belief

Vivekananda stressed the importance of self-confidence rooted in the recognition of one's own divine nature. He encouraged individuals to see beyond societal labels and limitations, embracing their intrinsic potential for greatness. This self-belief is fundamental for personal growth and empowerment, enabling individuals to pursue their goals with conviction and resilience.

2. Unity in Diversity

Vivekananda advocated for embracing diversity through compassion and empathy, emphasizing that true strength lies in unity. He taught that understanding and respecting differences can lead to a more harmonious and inclusive society, where each individual's contributions are valued and celebrated.

3. Education as Liberation

Vivekananda considered education to be a liberating force, essential for breaking free from ignorance and societal constraints. He championed an education system that not only imparts knowledge but also builds character and fosters moral values, empowering individuals to lead meaningful and autonomous lives.

4. The Role of Women in Society

Vivekananda was a strong proponent of women's empowerment, viewing women as pivotal nation builders. He believed that educating and empowering women changes the fabric of society, leading to greater progress and harmony. His teachings support the idea that empowered women are key to societal transformation.

5. Spiritual Foundations for Daily Living

Vivekananda emphasized the integration of spirituality into daily life. He suggested that spirituality should inform one's everyday actions and decisions, leading to a life that is not only personally fulfilling but also beneficial to others.

6. Overcoming Obstacles with Grace

Vivekananda taught that resilience and inner strength are crucial for overcoming life's challenges. He believed in facing adversity with courage and maintaining one's composure, viewing obstacles as opportunities for growth and learning.

7. The Virtue of Service

Service to others was central to Vivekananda's philosophy. He saw selfless service as a means to achieve spiritual growth and social change, emphasizing that true joy and fulfillment come from helping others and contributing to the community.

8. Leadership Inspired by Ethics

Vivekananda's teachings on leadership focus on ethical conduct and selflessness. He envisioned leaders as servants of the people, whose strength comes from moral integrity and the ability to inspire and uplift others.

9. Harmony of Mind and Body

Vivekananda advocated for maintaining balance between the mind and the body through practices such as yoga, meditation, and proper diet. He taught that a healthy body hosts a strong mind, and together they contribute to a holistic sense of well-being.

10. Inner Peace Through Meditation

Meditation is a key practice in Vivekananda's teachings for achieving inner peace and spiritual depth. He outlined methods to help individuals start meditating, emphasizing the transformative impact of regular meditation on personal and professional life.

11. Courage in the Face of Adversity

Vivekananda highlighted stories of bravery to inspire courage. He believed that courage based on spiritual faith and moral strength is essential to face and transcend difficulties.

12. The Joy of Giving

Generosity, according to Vivekananda, enriches the giver more than the receiver. He encouraged giving not just materialistically but also in terms of time, attention, and care, which fosters a happier and more cohesive society.

13. Fostering Community Spirit

Building supportive communities is crucial for individual and collective well-being. Vivekananda encouraged creating networks that provide mutual support, shared learning, and collective growth, enhancing community resilience and empowerment.

14. Mindfulness in Modern Times

Vivekananda's advice on mindfulness is especially pertinent today, as it helps individuals stay grounded and focused amid life's chaos. He provided practical tips for integrating mindfulness into daily activities, enhancing mental clarity and emotional stability.

15. Respecting Nature's Wisdom

Environmental consciousness was integral to Vivekananda's teachings, which call for respecting and preserving the natural world as part of spiritual practice. He saw this as essential for the health and well-being of both the planet and its inhabitants.

16. The Art of Communication

Effective communication, as taught by Vivekananda, is key to successful interpersonal relationships and leadership. He emphasized clarity, empathy, and honesty in all forms of communication, ensuring that messages are conveyed and received with integrity.

17. Cultivating Positive Relationships

Vivekananda believed that nurturing healthy relationships is essential for personal and social development. He provided guidelines for building trust, practicing empathy, and supporting mutual growth within relationships.

18. Empowerment Through Entrepreneurship

Encouraging women to engage in entrepreneurship is a powerful tool for empowerment. Vivekananda's ideals support women in using business ventures as platforms for achieving independence, expressing creativity, and impacting society positively.

19. Legacy of Kindness

In a competitive world, Vivekananda taught the importance of kindness and compassion. He believed that these qualities should pervade all aspects of life, influencing how individuals compete, lead, and succeed.

20. Vision for the Future

Inspiring a new generation of women leaders with Vivekananda's ideals involves instilling values of self-belief, ethical leadership, and community service. His vision empowers women to lead with strength, wisdom, and compassion, shaping a future where they play crucial roles in societal advancement.

In summary, Swami Vivekananda's teachings provide a rich framework for leading a balanced, ethical, and impactful life. His insights into personal development, leadership, and community engagement continue to inspire and guide individuals across the world, fostering a legacy of wisdom that transcends generations.

ᐅᐅᐅ

Citation And References

This book represents the culmination of extensive research and meticulous analysis, incorporating a diverse range of sources, including numerous books, scholarly studies, and personal experiences. Additionally, I have scoured various websites to gather relevant information and data essential for the compilation of this work. I have taken every precaution to ensure the accuracy of the information presented and have diligently cited all sources to acknowledge their contributions.

Despite these efforts, the possibility of inadvertent errors remains. I deeply value the insights of my readers and appreciate any feedback that can help identify and rectify such inaccuracies. I encourage you to bring any discrepancies to my attention.

Your feedback is not only welcome but crucial, as it will aid in correcting current editions and enhancing the content of future ones. I am committed to maintaining the highest standards of accuracy and reliability in my work and thank you for your support and understanding.

Additionally, I firmly uphold the principle of freedom of speech and expression as guaranteed under Article 19(1)(a) of the Constitution of India, and I respect the diverse viewpoints and expressions of all readers.

ррр

Other Books Of The Author

1. Empowering Minds: A Journey into Women's Self-Discovery and Power
2. The Dynamics of Motivation: Catalyzing Thought into Action
3. Meditation and Mental Well Being: The Path to Inner Peace and Clarity
4. The Psychology of Child Education: Nurturing Future Generations
5. Ethical Enlightenment: A Modern Guide to Living with Integrity
6. Voices of Empowerment: Stories of Women Rising Against Odds
7. Social Psychology in Everyday Life: Understanding Human Connections
8. The Essence of Motivational Speaking: Inspiring Change in Others
9. Balancing Acts: Women, Work, and the Will to Lead
10. Guiding with Grace: Raising Children with Compassion and Awareness
11. The Power of Positive Aging: Embracing Life After Fifty
12. Building Resilient Communities: Social Work in Action
13. The Ethical Educator: Principles for Teaching and Learning
14. From Insight to Impact: Social Psychology for a Better World
15. The Ethics of Empathy: A Guide to Ethical Living
16. The Science of Empowering the Self: Navigating Life's Challenges with Psychological Wisdom
17. The Mindful Conscious Leader: Meditation Techniques for Modern Management
18. Pioneering Spirit: Women's Pathways to Leadership and Empowerment
19. Feeling to Healing: The Role of Emotional Intelligence in Child Development
20. Transformative Talks and Words of Inspiration: Insights into Motivational Oratory

॥ ॥ ॥

Role of Social Media in Shaping Self-Esteem and Interpersonal Relationships among Adolescents

Dr. Minakshi Bansal
Social Activist
Ahmedabad, Gujarat, Bharat
minakshiindiag20@yahoo.com

❦❦❦

|| LOKAHA SAMASTHAHA SUKHINO BHAVANTU ||

• 137 •

www.ingramcontent.com/pod-product-compliance
Lightning Source LLC
Chambersburg PA
CBHW020839120726
48008CB00001B/20